BEAD
TATTING

by

Rosemarie
Peel

Contents

Introduction .....page 3
Equipment .....page 3
Bead sizing .....page 3
Abbreviations .....page 4
How to add beads .....pages 5/7
Before you begin .....page 8
Sue edging .....pages 8/9
Rolled hem .....page 10
Identity bracelet .....page 11
Liz edging .....page 12
Louise edging .....page 13
Bugle beads .....page 14
Ear-ring .....page 15
Gemstone spray .....pages 16/17
Helen edging .....pages 18/19
Barbara edging .....page 20
Claire edging .....page 21
Plants in pots .....pages 22/23
Butterfly bow .....pages 24/25
Sew-on motifs .....pages 26/27
Small triangle .....pages 28/29
Large triangle .....pages 30/32

Other books in this series:
TAT FIVE
YULETIDE TATTING

ISBN 1 874688 02 8

Printed in England by
Printhaus Graphique Ltd
Northampton.

First published in February 1993 by
Lacet Publications
29, St Nicolas Park Drive, Nuneaton, CV11 6DL

Introduction

'BEAD TATTING' contains patterns for all tatting enthusiasts who have mastered the basic techniques of the craft.

Beads give an extra dimension to tatting. They accentuate the design and add glitter, colour and weight. The patterns in this book have been specially designed to take full advantage of these extra qualities but, of course, beads can be incorporated in any tatting. If beads are used to add colour then their arrangement needs to be prominent and pleasing to the eye. If beads are used for their weight then gravity must be considered. I have made the mistake of adding beads to the top side of an edging only to find that it toppled over in use.

Use bead tatting to add sparkle to garments for special occasions such as a wedding, a party or a dance. A skirt or blouse with a beaded edging will hang better with the weight which beads provide. Why confine yourself to humans? A blaze could be made in bead tatting for a well-dressed horse! A weighty edging can also be used in furnishings such as along the bottom of curtains or around throw-overs from small sugar bowl covers to large chair covers.

Equipment

Apart from the beads, which are dealt with below, bead tatting takes little more than the usual tatting requirements of shuttles, thread and hook. However, as you develop the skills of bead tatting you will find that some types of equipment are preferable to others.

A fine crochet hook (size 0.60) is best for adding beads to No.20 crochet cotton or finer.

A fine beading needle is useful for putting the beads on the threads.

If the beads have small holes the thread won't fit through when doubled up on a needle. In this case rub some glue on the end of the thread and it will serve as the needle when dry.

A gauge should be used for making picots the right size, especially for adding the larger beads (size 4mm and over).

A tin lid or a tin tray with a rim keeps loose beads in check.

A good length of nail on your left-hand thumb is handy when working the next ds after a bead.

Some shuttles are better than others for holding beads and they may well not be your hitherto favourite ones. It takes much experience to load the beads onto a shuttle in just the right place for when they are needed. Consequently there will be plenty of undoing and doing up of the shuttle so choose one that does this with ease. Long bugle beads cannot be put on a spooled shuttle: one with a large fixed block middle is best.

Bead sizing

All the beads mentioned in this book have been measured in millimetres along the length of their drilled hole. These sizes are not critical but been chosen to match the thread used. The type of bead has been chosen for their position in the tatting. You can be flexible when sorting out which beads to use but always make sure you have enough. If you change the thickness of thread then change the bead size to match.

A 4mm bead could be square ⊟ or round ⊖
A bead with its top side drilled could be a drop or a leaf or a novelty.

Abbreviations

TATTING TERM and ABBREVIATION		EXPLANATION	DIAGRAM SYMBOLS
Double stitch	1, ds	The number denotes the quantity. Made up of two halves, plain and purl.	
Picot	-	Comes between whole ds. - (regular) - - (long)	
Chain	Ch	A number of ds made with the ball thread and sitting on the shuttle thread.	
Ring	R	A number of ds made using shuttle thread only.	
Close ring	close	Work continues from this close-up point on the ring.	
Reverse work	RW	The ring is tipped upside down before the next chain is made. Another RW tips it back.	
Join	+	A join is made to the appropriate free picot followed by a purl. This counts as the next ds.	
Lock join	LJ	Make this join with the shuttle thread in use at the time.	
Shuttle	Sh	Several in use are numbered to identify them.	with beads
Ball			with beads
Bead	b (see pp 5/7 for full details)	Various shapes depict beads; shaded grey in working diagrams and black in illustrations	

How to add beads

These three pages show ten ways in which beads can be worked into tatting. Refer to the box under each number to see how they are identified in the written pattern. Methods 1, 2, 3, and 4 use beads which have been put on the main shuttle thread. Method 7 uses beads on a second shuttle and methods 5 and 6 use beads which are on the ball thread or second shuttle. Methods 8, 9, and 10 do not need beads on the ball or shuttle threads.

1. On shuttle thread in place of picot in a ring

-b in ring instructions
plus a reminder (b?) at beginning of ring

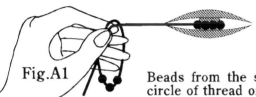

Beads from the shuttle must be enclosed in the circle of thread on your hand before you start the ring (Fig.A1). A reminder is placed in the written instructions so the pattern for this ring (Fig.A2) would read R(3b?) 5 -b 5 -b 5 -b 5 close.

2. On shuttle thread in a chain ──────

b
in chain
instructions

While working a chain, slide a bead along the shuttle thread and put it next to the last ds worked. The pattern for this chain (Fig.A3) would read Ch 3 b 2 b 3.

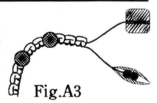

Fig.A3

3. On shuttle thread in a ring ──────

b
in ring
instructions

While working a ring, slide a bead along the shuttle thread and put it next to the last ds worked. The pattern for this ring (Fig.A4) would read R 3 b 3 b 3 b 3 close.

Fig.A4

4. On shuttle thread between rings. ──────

b
after a ring
is closed

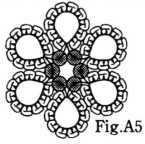

Fig.A5

Pass a bead along the shuttle thread up to a ring after it has been closed, start the next ring as close to the bead as possible. This is where a good nail on the left hand thumb is an asset. The pattern for Fig.A5 would read (R 6 - 6 close b) 6 times

5. On ball thread in place of picots on chains

| -b |
| in chain |
| instructions |

Pass a bead along the ball thread instead of making a picot in the appropriate place. The instructions for the chain shown in Fig.A6 would read Ch 2 -b 2 -b 2 -b 2 -b 2

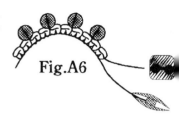

Fig.A6

6. On ball thread between chains

Fig.A7

| b |
| before the second chain |

Pass a bead along the ball thread after a chain. Either a ring (Fig.A7) or a lock join (Fig.A8) is worked before the bead is held in place by the next chain.

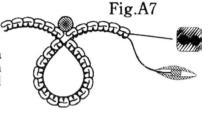

Fig.A8

7. On a second shuttle

Beads on a second shuttle can be placed as described in methods 1, 2, 3, 4, 5 and 6. The method described here is similar to method 1 so the beads need to be encased in the circle of thread round your hand before starting a ring (Fig.A1). By encasing quite a few beads but working just one ds in the ring a cluster of beads can be made to hang from a chain. The written instructions for Fig.A9 would read
Sh1: Ch 5 Sh2: R (5b?) 1 -bbbbb close Sh1: Ch 5.

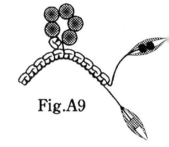

Fig.A9

8. Added with a hook when joining

| +b in written instructions |
| for rings and chains |

Make sure the appropriate picot is long enough to accommodate the bead. Put the bead on a hook, catch up the picot and slide the bead onto the picot (Fig.A10) before making the join as normal.

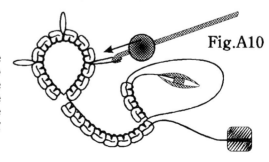

Fig.A10

9. Added with a hook at a free picot ─────

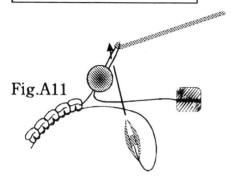

b+ in written instructions for rings and chains

Fig.A11

Put a bead on your hook, hook up the thread which is making the ds in a ring or chain, pass the bead onto the loop just formed, extend this loop so the shuttle can get through and the stitch can be completed (Fig.A11).

This way of adding beads at a picot is bulkier than the methods described in 1 and 5. The bead is firmly attached and so does not have the same freedom of movement. A forgotten bead from method 1 or 5 can be added in this way to save cutting the thread.

When adding a bead by method 8 or 9 you may come across one which is difficult to get on even the smallest of hooks. Put this bead on some fine thread, put this thread through the loop which is to hold the bead, then take it back through the bead (Fig.A12). Slide the bead along and the hook can then be inserted into the loop which is pulled through.

The difficult bead

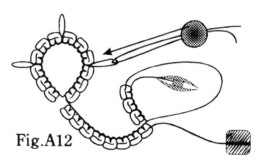

Fig.A12

10. Sewn on when mounting tatting ─────

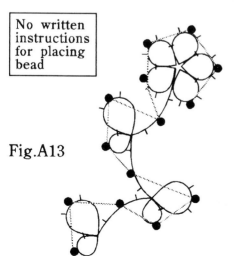

No written instructions for placing bead

Fig.A13

Most tatting can have beads sewn onto it when it is mounted onto fabric. Put the finished tatting in position and some matching thread on a needle. Starting from the back bring the needle up through the first picot which is to have a bead added. Put a bead on the needle and slide it onto the picot. Take the needle to the back of the fabric outside the picot. A little back stitch here would stop the work from puckering. Continue by coming up at the next picot. Fig.A13 shows the motif from page 26 with a grey line showing the route taken by the sewing thread.

Before you begin......

Bead tatting takes more thought and preparation than ordinary tatting so before you start working any pattern read it through. Make sure you know what is needed and where.

Sue

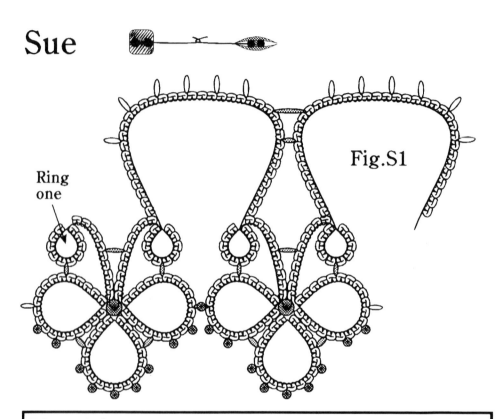

Ring one

Fig.S1

Materials
Fil a Dentelles No.80 cotton
Large beads - 4mm, 1 per repeat } creates the size illustrated in Fig.S2
Small beads - 2mm, 10 per repeat }

The working diagram (Fig.S1) shows two repeats of the pattern. Each repeat takes one large bead and ten small beads.

Before starting, have all the large beads needed on the ball thread. Put nine small beads of each repeat onto the shuttle thread, leaving the tenth to join at a picot with a hook.

Use the working diagram with the written instructions to see where the joins and beads are placed.

This edging curves slightly in on its chain side. Mount it on a circle of hemmed fabric (see page 10) or unhemmed net. A running stitch can be taken inside a hem or through the net, stopping at each free picot on the chain side to pick it up.

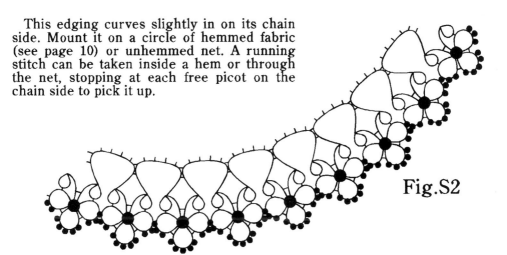

Fig.S2

Refer to page 6, method 6, for the large bead placement.
Refer to page 6, method 8, for the joined small bead.
Refer to page 5, method 1, for the small beads in the rings.

Fig,S1 Ring one 5 - 5 close, RW,
Ch 5 - 5, RW,
R(2b?) 5 + 5 - 2 -b 2 -b 2 - 4 close,
R(5b?) 4 + 2 -b 2 -b 2 -b 2 -b 2 - 4 close
R(2b?) 4 + 2 -b 2 -b 2 - 5 - 5 close, RW,
Pass a large bead along the ball thread and into position after the last chain.
b Ch 5 + 5, RW,
R 5 + 5 close, RW,
Ch 8 - 3 - 3 - 3 - 3 - 3 - 3 - 3 - 8, RW,
* R 5 - 5 close, RW,
Ch 5 - 5, RW,
On the next ring a small bead is added with a hook when joining the second picot to the adjacent ring.
R(2b?) 5 + 5 +b 2 -b 2 -b 2 - 4 close,
R(5b?) 4 + 2 -b 2 -b 2 -b 2 -b 2 - 4 close,
R(2b?) 4 + 2 -b 2 -b 2 - 5 - 5 close, RW,
Pass a large bead along the ball thread and into position after the last chain,
b Ch 5 + 5, RW,
R 5 + 5 close, RW,
Ch 8 + 3 + 3 - 3 - 3 - 3 - 3 - 3 - 8, RW,
Repeat from * for the required length. If the edging is to be made into a circle join the first and last trefoils together adding a small bead with a hook. Also join the last chain at its last two picots to the corresponding chain at the beginning. Fasten off the last chain to the close-up point of ring one.

HOW TO ROLL A CIRCULAR HEM

This example uses fine and closely woven fabric. The hem will be about 2.5mm deep. If your material is thicker or the weave is open, a bigger fold over will be needed. Adjust the measurements accordingly.

Referring to the diagram below:-
1) In pencil draw a circle on your fabric. Use a round template which fits inside your circular tatted edge, making allowance for the hem depth.
2) Cut away 8mm beyond the pencil line.
3) Fold 3mm of the fabric in all around using your finger and thumb to press.
4) Thread a needle and hide the end knot inside the fold line.
5) From where the thread comes out of the fold line go straight to the pencil line and make a tiny stitch.
6) Go diagonally back to the fold line and take a tiny stitch from there.
Repeat 5) and 6) four times, then, by pulling the sewing thread, the hem rolls over. Repeat this all the way round.

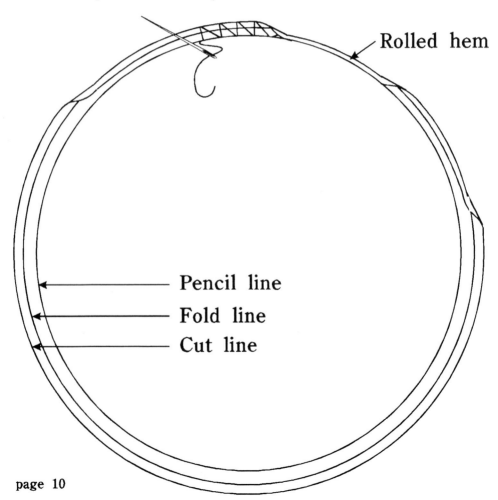

Rolled hem

Pencil line

Fold line

Cut line

Identity bracelet

Materials and

...Letter beads. (15 beads arranged into three words, with the chain spaces in between, make a bracelet length. Beads and chain spaces can be varied.)
...A boot button or similar.
...No 20 crochet cotton. (Black complements the letters on the beads)
...Strong silk thread used for making necklaces.
...Two shuttles wound equally onto opposite ends of 6 metres of the black cotton and named shuttle one (Sh1) and shuttle two (Sh2).
...One shuttle wound with 1 metre of the silk thread and named shuttle three (Sh3). Put all the beads in order and the right way up onto this silk thread before you start.

To start

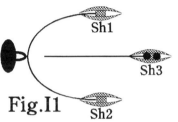

Fig.I1

Arrange the button and shuttles as shown in Fig.I1. Wind the end of silk thread (Sh3) three times through the button hole and round the black thread. Tie the silk thread in a reef knot close to the button hole and get rid of its end inside the ds of the following chain.

Holding the threads from Sh1 and Sh2 together to form thick stitches,
Sh3: Ch 8
A letter bead will be passed along to lie next to the last chain.
Taking Sh2 thread behind Sh3 arrange all as in Fig.I2.

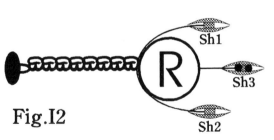

Fig.I2

* Sh1: (R 5 close,) twice, RW,
Sh2: (R 5 close,) twice, RW
Pull the following two ds up as tight as possible to hold a bead from Sh3 in place.
Sh3: Ch 1 (with Sh1 thread,) RW,
Sh3: Ch 1 (with Sh2 thread,) RW.
Repeat from * to the end of the word then hold the two black threads together, Sh3: Ch 6.

Make the button loop at the end of the bracelet, using the silk thread on Sh3 to make a large enough ring. Close this ring and wind the silk end round to lie with it. Cut 40cm of black thread away from the other two shuttles, thread them both on one needle and blanket stitch round the silk loop before sewing in the two black ends separately.

Liz

This simple little edging looks particularly effective in a random die thread.

I used DMC Fil a Dentelles No.80 thread with 5mm silver lined bugle beads (1 per repeat) and 2mm silver lined rocailles (3 per repeat) each repeat measuring just over 1cm. In these proportions it makes a weighty little edging, very suitable for a drinking glass or sugar bowl cover. Refer to page 10 for preparing the circular fabric on which to mount it.

Fig.L1

Put all the small beads needed on the ball thread then keep sliding the beads along as you wind up the shuttle. These will be put in the place of picots in the chains (see page 6 method 5).

Make the long picots in the rings 5mm long to accommodate the bugle beads which are added with a hook (see page 6 method 8). The first long picot on ring one is for adding a bead on the last ring if the edging is to be made into a round.

Refer to Fig.L1 and with ball and shuttle thread:-

Ring one 3 - 3 - - 3 - 3 - 3 - 3 - - 3 - 3 close, RW,

* Ch 3 - 3 -b 3 - 3 -b 3 - 3 -b 3 - 3, RW,

R 3 - 3 +b 3 - 3 - 3 - 3 - - 3 - 3 close, RW,

Repeat from * for any sized round then make the last ring

R 3 - 3 +b 3 - 3 - 3 - 3 +b 3 - 3 close, RW,

Ch 3 - 3 -b 3 - 3 -b 3 - 3 -b 3 - 3.

Fasten off to the close-up point on Ring one.

Fig.L2

Louise

Materials

This edging is designed for large drop beads with their top sides drilled. One bead is required per repeat of the pattern. It is added with a hook (see page 7, method 9).

Worked in No.20 crochet cotton this edging is the size shown in Fig.L4, it will curve on its ring side if necessary.

Refer to Fig.L3 which shows one repeat of the pattern.

With ball and shuttle thread:-
Ring one 2 - 2 - 2 - 2 - 2 - 5 - 5 close, RW,
Ch 6, RW,
R 4 + 4 - 4 - 4 close, RW,
Ch 2 - 2 - 2 - 2, RW,
R 4 + 4 - 4 - 4 close, RW,
Ch 2 - 2 - 2 - 2, RW,
R 2 + 2 - 4 close, RW,
Ch 2 - 2 b+ 2 - 2, LJ to the free picot on the previous ring,
(Ch 2 - 2 - 2 - 2, LJ to the free picot on the next ring up) twice
Ch 2 - 2 - 2 - 2 - 2, RW,
R 10 + 2 - 2 - 2 - 2 - 2 close,
Repeat from the beginning for the length required.

To straighten the final edge (Fig.L4), omit the last ring and make the last chain, Ch 6, LJ to the next free picot up.

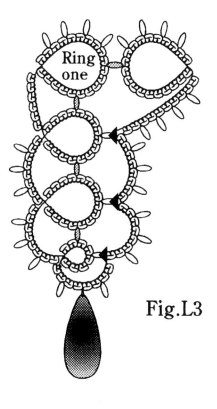

Fig.L3

Fig.L4

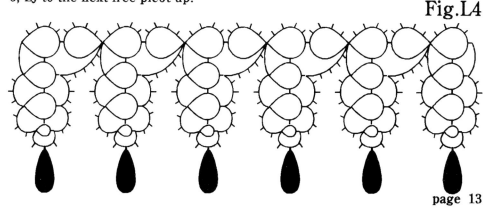

Bugle beads

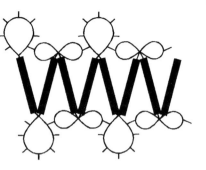

There is a tortoiseshell shuttle available which has a large cuboid centre and is ideal for bead tatting, especially this edging which needs to have long beads on the shuttle thread.

Bugle beads are long rocailles and as such make the tatting heavy. This edging (illustrated above, to scale) is worked in No 20 crochet cotton with bugle beads which are 15mm long. There are four beads to each repeat of this pattern and, using the shuttle which is recommended, it is possible to load on enough beads for 8 repeats. Space each of the beads between a large ring's length of thread when winding up the shuttle.

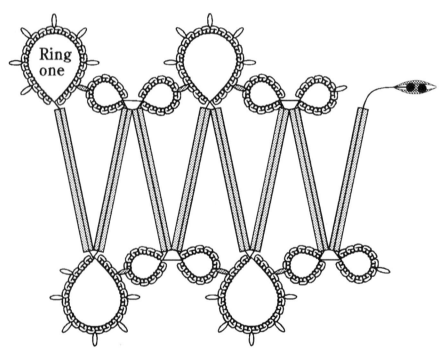

With shuttle thread loaded with the bugle beads:-
Ring one 3 - 3 - 3 - 3 - 3 - 3 - 3 - 3 close, RW,
Pass a bead up to the last ring and start the next ring close to its other end.
R 3 - 3 - 3 - 3 - 3 - 3 - 3 - 3 close, RW, pass bead along as before,
*(R 6 + 6 close, R 6 - 6 close, RW, pass bead along as before) twice,
(R 3 + 3 - 3 - 3 - 3 - 3 - 3 - 3 close RW, pass bead along as before) twice.
Repeat from * for the length required.

Ear-ring

Materials per ear-ring

Ear-ring finding for pierced ear or clip-on finding or screw-on finding.
No.20 crochet cotton.
38 beads - 2mm

Fig.E1

This is quite simply a spiral of twelve rings. The beads are positioned on the outside edge of the spiral. Fig.E1 gives some idea of what it will look like. REMEMBER to enclose the beads in the circle of thread round your hand every time a ring is made. See page 5, method 1.
With all the beads on the shuttle thread:-
Fig.E2, Ring one (3b?) 4 - 2 -b 2 -b 2 -b 2 - 4 close,
[R (3b?) 4 + 2 -b 2 -b 2 -b 2 - 4 close] 10 times
R (5b?) 4 + 2 -b 2 -b 2 -b 2 -b 2 -b 2 close
Sew in ends.
Hang onto the finding by the first picot worked.
Make a second ear-ring to match.

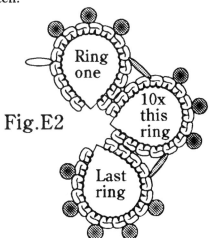

Fig.E2

Ring one

10x this ring

Last ring

Experiment with this idea, this ear-ring is so quick to make there will not be much wasted time. Try any thread, any beads and vary the number and size of the rings.

Gemstone spray

This spray is designed so that special beads can be displayed to their full advantage. It is made up of two layers, the leaves and the flower, which are held together with a central large bead. When completed it can be used as a brooch or hair decoration.

Materials	These give the approximate size shown
No.20 crochet cotton	in Figs.G2, G3, and G5. They can be
20 small beads - 2mm	scaled up or down according to the
10 medium beads - 4mm	beads and thread available. Also more
1 large bead - at least 8mm	small and medium beads can be used
	for a fuller flower.

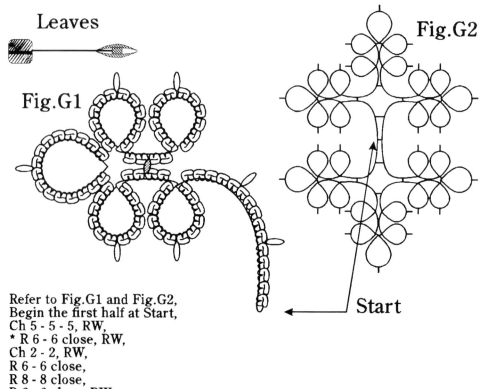

Leaves

Fig.G1

Fig.G2

Start

Refer to Fig.G1 and Fig.G2,
Begin the first half at Start,
Ch 5 - 5 - 5, RW,
* R 6 - 6 close, RW,
Ch 2 - 2, RW,
R 6 - 6 close,
R 8 - 8 close,
R 6 - 6 close, RW,
Ch 2 + 2, RW,
R 6 - 6 close, RW,
Ch 5 + 5 - 5, RW,
Repeat from * two more times joining the last picot of the last repeat to the first picot made.
A picot starts the second half which is a repeat of the first half.
To finish, cut the threads and sew one through the starting point and its adjacent picot. Tie the ends in a reef knot but do not sew them in as they are used to assemble the spray (Fig.G5).

page 16

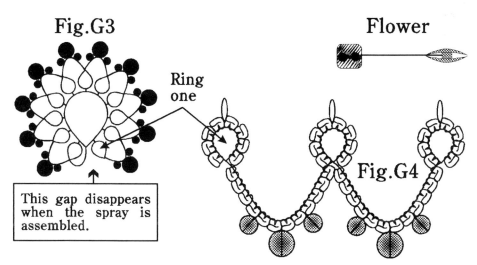

Fig.G3

Flower

Ring one

> This gap disappears when the spray is assembled.

Fig.G4

Onto the ball thread put one small bead, one medium bead, one small bead, ten times (or more if you want a fuller flower). Then keep sliding the beads along as you wind up the shuttle.
Refer to Figs.G3 and G4.
Ring one 4 - 4 close, RW,
Ch 4 -b 2 -b 2 -b 4, RW,
Repeat this ring and chain ten times. (or more if required)
R 4 - 4 close, RW, Ch 8, RW,
The next ring gathers up, in order, all the previous rings by their picots, starting with the last (adding more +2's if required).
R 1+ 2 + 2 + 2 + 2 + 2 + 2 + 2 + 2 + 2 + 1 close.
Cut, tie and sew in ends.

The assembled spray

Use the ends from the completed leaves to hold the whole spray together. Take them through the large central ring of the flower (Fig.G3), through the large bead, then back again to attach a pin or clip mount. Fig.G5 gives some idea of what the finished spray will look like.

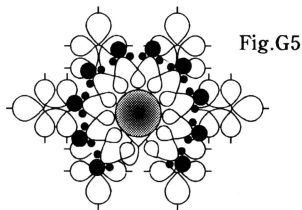

Fig.G5

Helen

Beads are only added to the Helen edging when rows of it are made up into a solid area of tatting as illustrated opposite.
First make the Helen edging according to the length required, either horizontally or vertically across an area.
When joining the chain edges together add beads at the central five picots on each chain. Follow the alternative instructions in the [ ] brackets.
When joining the ring edges together add beads to the two picots on each ring which are not joined within the edging. Follow the alternative instructions in the ( ) brackets.

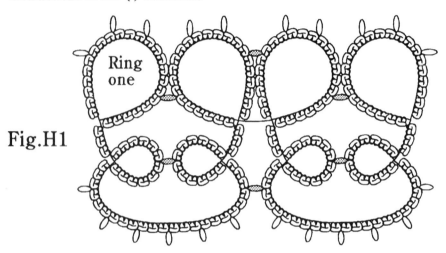

Ring
one

Fig.H1

With ball and shuttle thread and referring to Fig.H1:
Ring one 6 - 3 - 3 - 6 - 6 close, (or R 6 - 3 +b 3 +b 6 - 6 close)
RW, Ch 3, RW,
R 6 - 6 close, RW,
Ch 3 - 3 - 3 - 3 - 3 - 3 - 3 - 3, [or Ch 3 - 3 +b 3 +b 3 +b 3 +b 3 +b 3 - 3]
RW, * R 6 + 6 close, RW,
Ch 3, RW,
R 6 + 6 - 3 - 3 - 6 close, (or R 6 + 6 +b 3 +b 3 - 6 close)
R 6 + 3 - 3 - 6 - 6 close, (or R 6 + 3 +b 3 +b 6 - 6 close)
RW, Ch 3, RW,
R 6 - 6 close, RW,
Ch 3 + 3 - 3 - 3 - 3 - 3 - 3 - 3, RW, [or Ch 3 + 3 +b 3 +b 3 +b 3 +b 3 +b 3 - 3]
Repeat from * for the length required.
Round the edging off with the next two rings of the pattern and the chain between.

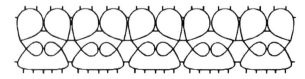

Materials - No.20 crochet cotton and 2mm beads make the Helen edging the size illustrated below. It is joined in vertical rows. See page 6, method 8 for how to add beads with a hook when making a join.

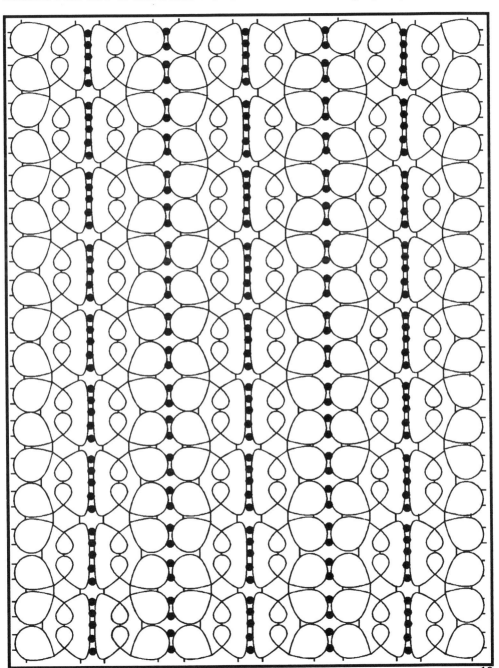

Barbara

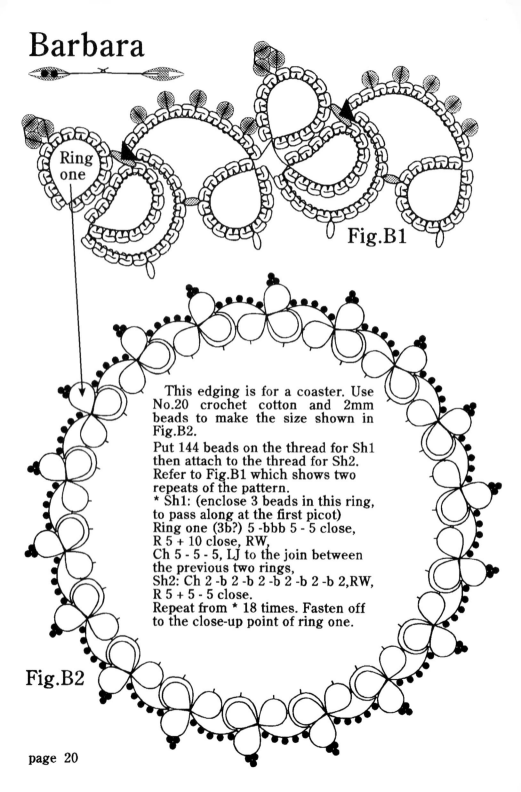

Fig.B1

Ring one

Fig.B2

This edging is for a coaster. Use No.20 crochet cotton and 2mm beads to make the size shown in Fig.B2.

Put 144 beads on the thread for Sh1 then attach to the thread for Sh2. Refer to Fig.B1 which shows two repeats of the pattern.

* Sh1: (enclose 3 beads in this ring, to pass along at the first picot)
Ring one (3b?) 5 -bbb 5 - 5 close,
R 5 + 10 close, RW,
Ch 5 - 5 - 5, LJ to the join between the previous two rings,
Sh2: Ch 2 -b 2 -b 2 -b 2 -b 2 -b 2,RW,
R 5 + 5 - 5 close.
Repeat from * 18 times. Fasten off to the close-up point of ring one.

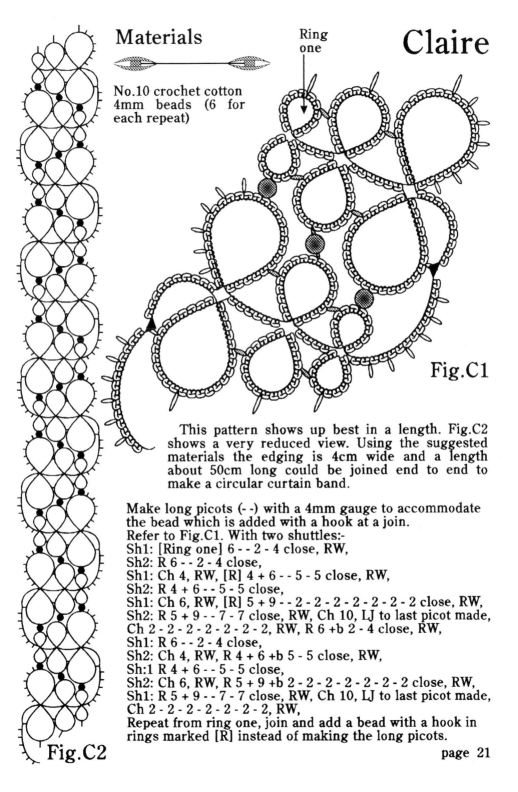

Materials

No.10 crochet cotton
4mm beads (6 for
each repeat)

Ring one

Claire

Fig.C1

Fig.C2

This pattern shows up best in a length. Fig.C2 shows a very reduced view. Using the suggested materials the edging is 4cm wide and a length about 50cm long could be joined end to end to make a circular curtain band.

Make long picots (- -) with a 4mm gauge to accommodate the bead which is added with a hook at a join.
Refer to Fig.C1. With two shuttles:-
Sh1: [Ring one] 6 - - 2 - 4 close, RW,
Sh2: R 6 - - 2 - 4 close,
Sh1: Ch 4, RW, [R] 4 + 6 - - 5 - 5 close, RW,
Sh2: R 4 + 6 - - 5 - 5 close,
Sh1: Ch 6, RW, [R] 5 + 9 - - 2 - 2 - 2 - 2 - 2 - 2 - 2 close, RW,
Sh2: R 5 + 9 - - 7 - 7 close, RW, Ch 10, LJ to last picot made,
Ch 2 - 2 - 2 - 2 - 2 - 2 - 2, RW, R 6 +b 2 - 4 close, RW,
Sh1: R 6 - - 2 - 4 close,
Sh2: Ch 4, RW, R 4 + 6 +b 5 - 5 close, RW,
Sh:1 R 4 + 6 - - 5 - 5 close,
Sh2: Ch 6, RW, R 5 + 9 +b 2 - 2 - 2 - 2 - 2 - 2 - 2 close, RW,
Sh1: R 5 + 9 - - 7 - 7 close, RW, Ch 10, LJ to last picot made,
Ch 2 - 2 - 2 - 2 - 2 - 2 - 2, RW,
Repeat from ring one, join and add a bead with a hook in rings marked [R] instead of making the long picots.

Plants in pots

This is a fun edging (Fig.P4 illustrates it in miniature), quick to work for the area it covers. The personal choice of beads and thread can create many colourful variations.

I used No.40 crochet cotton. The small beads are 2mm rocailles and the large cube bead is 1cm. Fig.P2 shows the scale.

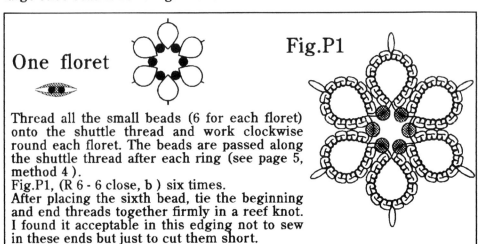

One floret

Fig.P1

Thread all the small beads (6 for each floret) onto the shuttle thread and work clockwise round each floret. The beads are passed along the shuttle thread after each ring (see page 5, method 4).

Fig.P1, (R 6 - 6 close, b) six times.

After placing the sixth bead, tie the beginning and end threads together firmly in a reef knot. I found it acceptable in this edging not to sew in these ends but just to cut them short.

One plant is made up of 7 florets

Refer to Fig.P2. Work the florets in the order shown and join them to each other on the rings whose picots touch. All the picots in floret No.1 are joined to twice. Start each floret with an unjoined ring then make the two, three or four joins as necessary. In florets 3 and 4 the rings marked (x) each have an extra picot 12mm long (use a gauge) so the details are:-

Floret 3, R(x) 5 - - 1 - 6 close
Floret 4, R(x) 6 + 1 - - 5 close

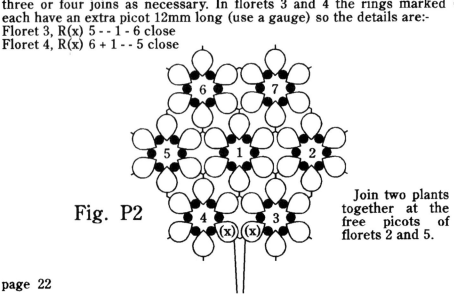

Fig. P2

Join two plants together at the free picots of florets 2 and 5.

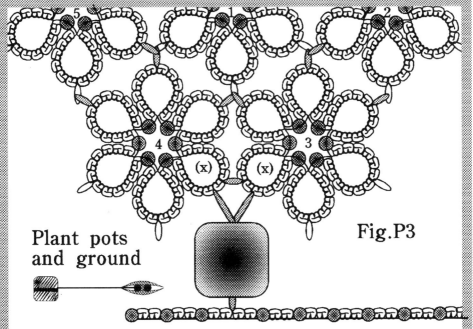

Plant pots and ground

Fig.P3

Fig.P3 shows the lower half of a plant in a pot, which is a large bead, on the ground, which is a beaded chain.

For each plant 1 large bead and an average of 12 small beads are needed. The large beads are added with a hook. Put all the small beads on the shuttle thread to be passed along into the chain at every 'b'.

With the ball thread continuous with the shuttle thread hold onto the first small bead from the shuttle thread to start the chain:-

* Ch b 2 b 2 b 2 +b (place a large bead on a hook, hook up both the long picots of the first bush, push the large bead along onto them and then complete the join).

Continue Ch 2 b 2 b 2 b 2 b 2 b 2 b 2 b 2 b 2 b 2. Keep repeating this chain from * for each bush, stopping 6 beads short on the last repeat.

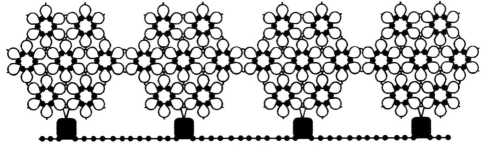

Fig.P4 - four potted plants in a row.

Butterfly bow

Materials

This pattern takes exactly 362 little beads. I used 2mm rocailles with No.20 crochet cotton to make the size shown in Fig.B5. It looks spectacular when gold thread and many coloured beads are used.

A 6ml (one level teaspoon) measure will give you enough of these beads.

As there are so many beads needed and not much shuttle thread it is better to use a needle than a shuttle. Have all the beads on a tray in front of you and pick them up with the needle when required.

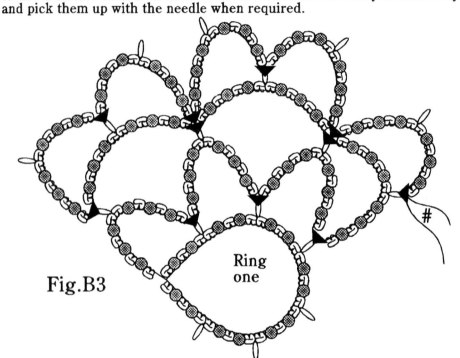

Fig.B3

Ring one

\#

With a needle on the ball thread make a ring an arm's length away from the needle. Use the needle in the same way you would a shuttle. At every 'b' in the written instructions thread a bead on the needle and put it in position by the last ds. (refer to Fig.B3)

Ring one 1 b 1 b 1 - 1 b 1 b 1 - 1 b 1 b 1 - 1 b 1 b 1 - 1 b 1 b 1 - 1 b 1 b 1 - 1 b 1 b 1 close, RW,

(Ch 1 b 1 b 1 b 1 - 1 b 1 b 1 b 1, LJ to the next picot on ring one) 3 times.

Turn the work sideways (i.e. towards you and to the left) and make a reverse stitch (this is the first half of the ds pulled up like a single knot so that the ball and shuttle threads change position).

(Ch 1 b 1 b 1 b 1 - 1 b 1 b 1 b 1, LJ to the next chain's picot) 3 times.

Turn the work sideways and make a reverse stitch as before.

(Ch 1 b 1 b 1 b 1 - 1 b 1 b 1 b 1, LJ to the next chain's picot,

Ch 1 b 1 b 1 b 1 - 1 b 1 b 1 b 1, LJ through the next LJ of the previous row and the picot to which it is joined) twice.

Ch 1 b 1 b 1 b 1 - 1 b 1 b 1 b 1, LJ to the next chain's picot.

You are now at \# on Fig.B3.

Continue with three more rows thus:-

{Turn the work sideways and make a reverse stitch
{(Ch 1 b 1 b 1 b 1 - 1 b 1 b 1 b 1, LJ to the next chain's picot) 5 times} twice

Turn the work sideways and make a reverse stitch
(Ch 1 b 1 b 1 b 1 b 1 b 1 b 1, LJ to the next chain's picot) 5 times.
Cut and sew in ends. This completes Fig.B4, the first half.

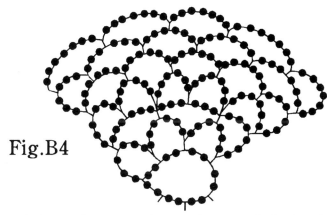

Fig.B4

Make the second half of the butterfly as the first half but join the
preliminary ring of the second half to the first three picots of ring one.
Make sure that the second half is a mirror image of the first by having the
close-up points of both rings facing the same way. The first of these joins is
where the antennae are attached (Fig.B5).

Antennae

With a needle on the end of the ball thread,
pick up a bead and start a chain with it.
Ch b 1 b 1 b 1 b 1 b 1 b 1 LJ to the butterfly,
Ch 1 b 1 b 1 b 1 b 1 b 1 b 1. Sew in ends.

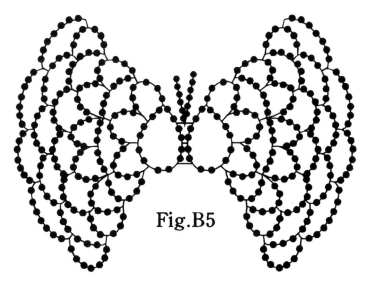

Fig.B5

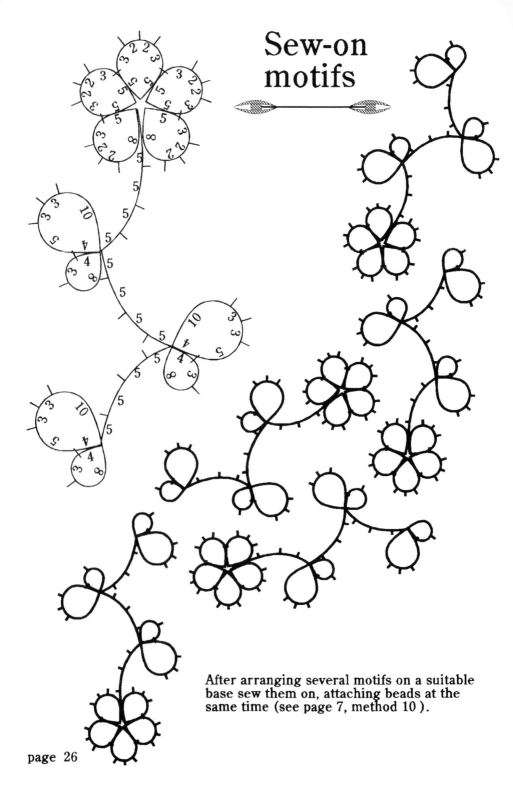

Sew-on motifs

After arranging several motifs on a suitable base sew them on, attaching beads at the same time (see page 7, method 10).

This motif is made up entirely of 5ds sections.
The first six single rings are 5 x 5ds.
They are on a chain which has 6 x 5ds.
The rings in the trefoils have 4 x 5ds.
The rings from the pairs have 2 x 5ds.
All the picoted chains are 4 x 5ds.

Small triangle

This triangle, on its own, is a corner or can be a decorative end to an epaulette or belt. Repeated in a line it makes a weighty fringe (Fig.T3), which would look good on a lampshade. The triangle can be mirrored to make a diamond shape (Fig.T4) to be used as a flash, a blaze or a teardrop.

Materials

No 40 crochet cotton
13 beads - 4mm } Creates the size shown in Fig.T2

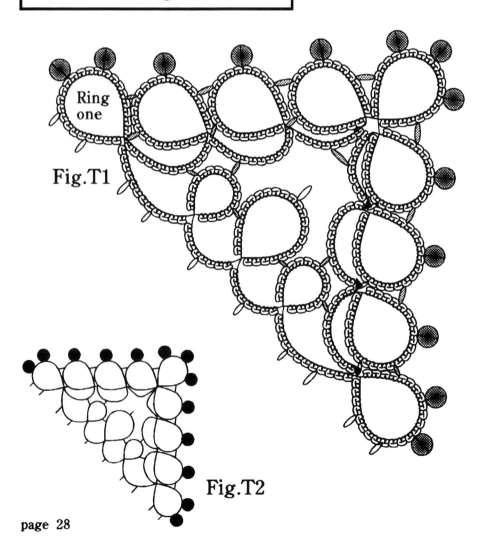

Ring one

Fig.T1

Fig.T2

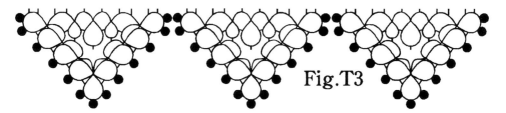

Fig.T3

Put all the beads (13 for each triangle) on Sh1.
Refer to Fig.T1
Sh1: Ring one (2b?) 4 - 4 - 4 -b 4 -b 4 - 4 close, RW,
Ch 8 - 4, RW,
On the next three rings make the first join to the close-up point of the previous ring.
R (1b?) 8 + 4 + 4 -b 4 - 4 close, RW,
Ch 4 - 8, RW,
R (1b?) 8 + 4 + 4 -b 4 - 4 close, RW,
Ch 4 - 4, RW,
R (1b?) 8 + 4 + 4 -b 4 - 4 close,
R (3b?) 4 + 4 -b 4 -b 4 - 4 close,
R (1b?) 4 + 4 -b 4 - 4 - 8 close, RW,

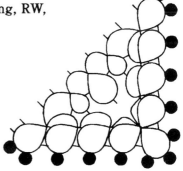

Ch 4 + 4, LJ to the last picot on the previous ring, RW,
R (1b?) 4 + 4 -b 4 - 4 - 8 close, RW,
Ch 8 - 4, LJ as before, RW,
R (1b?) 4 + 4 -b 4 - 4 - 8 close, RW,
Ch 4 - 8, LJ as before, RW,
R (2b?) 4 + 4 -b 4 -b 4 - 4 - 4 close,
Sh2: Ch 4 - 4 - 4, RW,
R 4 + 4 + 4 - 4 close, RW, Ch 4 - 4, RW,
R 4 + 8 - 8 - 4 close, RW, Ch 4 - 4, RW,
R 4 + 4 + 4 + 4 close, RW, Ch 4 - 4 - 4,
Fasten off to the close-up point of Ring one.

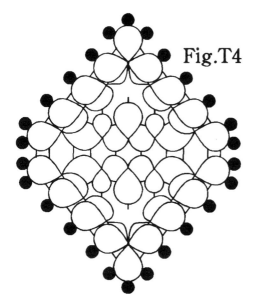

Fig.T4

Join two triangles at all their free picots along their unbeaded sides to make the diamond shape in Fig.T4. The close of this motif is a bit tricky so stick to my golden rule and keep the ring or chain being worked to the front (i.e. facing the shuttle in use). Keep the completed tatting, containing the picots which are going to be joined, to the back or underneath. You will know if you have done it wrong because you will either get your threads trapped or a joined picot will be twisted, or both!

Large triangle

The body of the triangle is worked first, in continuous rows from side to side. The beaded edging, shown in Fig.T7 with a heavy line, is put on afterwards, the instructions being overleaf.

With the use of a large shuttle it would be possible to make a woollen shawl by basing the triangle on a first row which is one metre long.

In this pattern chains face in opposite directions suggesting the use of two shuttles. However use just one shuttle with the ball thread and you will see after a few rows that the tatting eases into shape.

A neat touch is to remember to keep the ball thread on the same side of the work as it passes across the two adjacent rings.

To start the first row

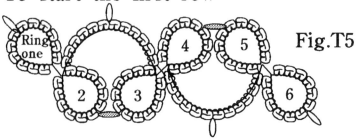

Fig.T5

The working diagram, Fig.T5, shows how the body of the triangle starts. These six rings are the first ones numbered in Fig.T7.

With ball and shuttle thread:-
Ring one 6 - 6 close, RW,
R 6 - 6 close, RW,
* Ch 6 - 6, RW, (successive chains face in opposite directions.)
R 6 + 6 close, RW,
R 6 - 6 close, RW,
Repeat from * to make the triangle as big as you want. For Fig.T7 it was eight times finishing with ring 18.

The row end on the right

Fig.T6, Ch 6 - 6, RW,
R(No.19) 6 + 6 close, RW,
(Future rows have an extra ring here, R 6 + 6)
Ch 6 - 6, RW,
R(No.20) 6 + 6 close, RW,
R(No.21) 6 - 6 close,
Ch 6 - 6, RW,
R(No.22) 6 + 6 close, RW,
Refer to Fig. T7 and continue along the row joining where necessary.

Extra ring on all rows except the first

Fig.T6

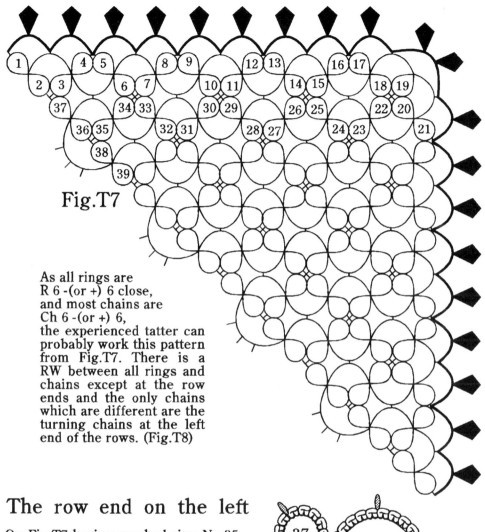

Fig.T7

As all rings are
R 6 -(or +) 6 close,
and most chains are
Ch 6 -(or +) 6,
the experienced tatter can
probably work this pattern
from Fig.T7. There is a
RW between all rings and
chains except at the row
ends and the only chains
which are different are the
turning chains at the left
end of the rows. (Fig.T8)

The row end on the left

On Fig.T7 having reached ring No.35,
follow Fig.T8 in numerical order.
Ch 6 + 6, RW,
R(No.36) 6 + 6 close, RW,
R(No.37) 6 + 6 close,
Ch 6 - 3 - 3 - 6, RW,
R(No.38) 6 + 6 close, RW,
R(No.39) 6 - 6 close, RW,

Complete the triangle with ever
decreasing rows referring to Fig.T7,
then add the beaded edging following
the instructions at the top of page 32.

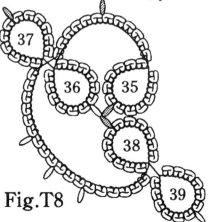

Fig.T8

Beaded edging for the large triangle

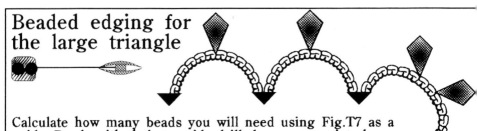

Calculate how many beads you will need using Fig.T7 as a guide. Beads with their top side drilled are appropriate here. Put them all on the ball thread then wind up the shuttle.

Lock join to the picot on Ring one,
Ch 6 -b 6, LJ to the picot on the next chain.
Ch 6 -b 6, LJ to the join between the next two rings along.
Continue along both sides in this manner but include the corner chain:- Ch 6 -b 2 -b 6, LJ to the picot on the next chain.

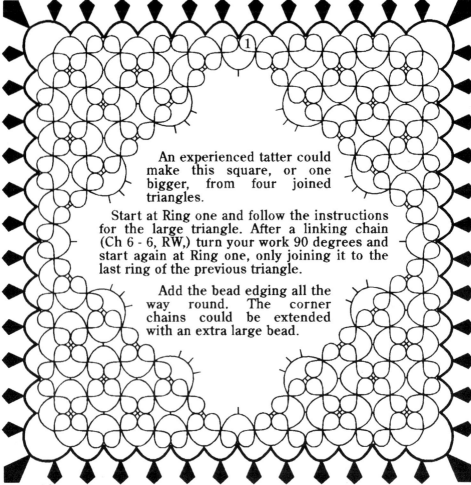

An experienced tatter could make this square, or one bigger, from four joined triangles.

Start at Ring one and follow the instructions for the large triangle. After a linking chain (Ch 6 - 6, RW,) turn your work 90 degrees and start again at Ring one, only joining it to the last ring of the previous triangle.

Add the bead edging all the way round. The corner chains could be extended with an extra large bead.